A Taste of
Chicken Soup for the Soul®

Think Positive

*Inspirational Stories about Counting Your
Blessings and Having a Positive Attitude*

Jack Canfield
Mark Victor Hansen
Amy Newmark

Chicken Soup for the Soul Publishing, LLC
Cos Cob, CT

A Taste of Chicken Soup for the Soul: Think Positive
Inspirational Stories about Counting Your Blessings and Having
a Positive Attitude
Jack Canfield, Mark Victor Hansen & Amy Newmark

Published by Chicken Soup for the Soul Publishing, LLC
www.chickensoup.com

The publisher gratefully acknowledges the many publishers and
individuals who granted Chicken Soup for the Soul permission to
reprint the cited material.

Front cover photo courtesy of iStockphoto.com/Irochka_T
(© Irina Tischenko).

Library of Congress Control Number: 2010930826

A Taste of ISBN: 978-1-61159-865-0

Full Book ISBN: 978-1-935096-56-6

Contents

Two Strangers

My charmed life has been full of humorous moments — tidbits for laughable dinner table conversations with friends. I've noticed that often my life stories begin with the words "Guess what happened to me," followed by stories of horrible dates or embarrassing situations. While comical and entertaining, none of these moments have held great significance or importance. I didn't realize that a truly profound moment was heading my way one humid day in July when my car broke down in St. Joseph, Michigan.

A mere seven weeks before this breakdown, I left Michigan after walking out of a meaningless job, heading to Colorado to begin a new life and career at the age of twenty-six. I felt deeply that this was my chance to make my way in the world — living out a dream working with kids at the YMCA in Colorado Springs.

This dreamed "new life" never happened. Instead, I spent four of the seven weeks sick before facing the fact that the altitude did not agree with my asthma. Forced to leave what I thought was my new, exciting life, I faced the unpleasant reality of returning to my ho-hum existence in Michigan where my life status would read: twenty-six-year-old woman, single, unemployed, living at home with parents and no idea what to do with her life.

Driving 1,400 miles alone, sick and down-in-the-dumps was awful, although the word "awful" doesn't fully describe how bad the reality was. The constant wheezing, shortness of breath, and heavy pain in my lungs caused me extreme discomfort and the medication I consumed made me constantly drowsy.

Relief appeared as I reached the Michigan border at about 10:00 PM. Tired and facing a four-hour drive, I pulled off in the town of St. Joseph, rented a room at a motel, and immediately went to bed. I hadn't noticed the exhaust fan in my car was still running as I walked into the hotel. I definitely noticed when my car wouldn't start the next morning.

At that minute, in the parking lot of the motel, I wanted to cry. I wanted to scream. On top of all of the medical and mental stress heaped on me over the past seven weeks, I now had to tackle not only a physical breakdown, but also a car breakdown. I just wanted to be home. Home. But here I was — stuck, sick, tired of driving, mad at having to leave opportunity behind, and mad at the world. I've grown up listening to people tell me that, "God never gives us more than we can handle." It seems in moments like these that He likes to push the envelope.

After a tow to the nearest dealership, I settled in the waiting room for a two-hour repair. That's when I started talking to an older woman who sat a few chairs away from me.

She had a friendly face lined softly with wisdom, and an approachable, motherly look.

"So you're having some repairs done?" she asked with concern in her voice. I guessed she could see the frustration on my face.

"Yes," I said with a sigh. "My car wouldn't start. I have no idea what happened." I leaned back in my seat, put my head back against the blank wall behind me and stared up at the dull, fluorescent lights on the ceiling contemplating how many hours I would be sitting there.

That's when unexpectedly, unknown to me, and at the strangest time, my significant moment began to unfold. It began normally as this kind lady and I started to talk. She asked me to tell her about what happened to my car. I did, and then we settled into comfortable, casual conversation — the stuff you talk about with strangers in waiting rooms like vacations, the history of weather in Michigan, and places to eat. Then our conversation shifted from the obscure to more personal things. She talked about her struggle with feelings of guilt as she contemplated putting her eighty-five-year-old mother in a nursing home. I tried to sympathize and told her how my parents, themselves into their sixties, were talking about getting insurance in case one or both wound up needing nursing home care. We talked about life — real life. We talked about my trip to Colorado, my asthma, her home, her husband retiring, my parents retiring.

"Your car is ready ma'am," said the service manager to the woman.

"Oh, thank you," she said.

She stood up and I smiled at her. She wished me luck as she gathered her purse and car keys from the seat next to her. But then as she was about to walk away, she hesitated and then turned back to me.

"You know, I have to tell you something," she said, and I could see a serious expression color her face. The brightness in her blue eyes dimmed a bit as she glanced at the floor and then looked straight into my eyes. "My daughter died a few years ago. It's so hard even now to do just the simple things." She swallowed hard, exhaled deeply and went on, "But every now and then I meet someone who reminds me of my daughter, and today, you reminded me so much of her." She smiled with tears in her eyes and went on. "I believe that some-times God puts people in my path to remind me of her and to show me that my daughter is still with me and that I can get through this. I've so enjoyed talking to you today." A gen-uine smile covered her face. "When you get home I want you to hug your parents. They are very lucky to have you."

I gulped down an enormous lump in my throat. I didn't know how to respond. I felt tears of my own welling up in my eyes, and all I managed was to mumble a lame-sounding, "Oh gosh, thank you." I was dumbfounded, confused, and most of all sad. I felt so moved by what she said, so touched by this revelation about her daughter and the whole-hearted sentiment she put into telling me this. I'm a person who normally hides my emotions, but that day I stood up and hugged her and said, "I enjoyed talking to you too," and I meant it.

A few hours later, I pulled into the driveway at my parents' house. My mom came outside with her usual broad, inviting smile, and she wrapped me in a huge hug — the kind that generates love and warmth that only a mom can give. I was home. I hugged my mom with all my might. Since that day I've never questioned why bad things, crazy things, funny things, or just plain everything sometimes happen to me. And I'll certainly never ask "why me" when I have car trouble again.

~Maggie Koller

Finding the Real Me

It started out as one of the best days of my life, and certainly, of my career. My staff and I had been named the number one unit in our company, and I was taking them out for a celebratory lunch. I worked with a wonderful group of people and we were proud of what our hard work and team spirit had accomplished during the prior year.

Lunch was fun, the food excellent, and the camaraderie at the table made me smile. I was proud of this group, who laughed, cried, and loved each other, and I felt blessed to be their leader. The weather was crisp, cool, and sunny, and I thought to myself "it just doesn't get any better than this." It was a perfect day.

After lunch, we returned to work. As I

checked my e-mail, an urgent message popped up for a mandatory teleconference later that afternoon. We had these types of teleconferences quite a bit to cut costs versus expensive management meetings, so I thought nothing of it and continued to catch up on work and phone calls I had missed during lunch.

Two o'clock came — time for the teleconference. I put my phone on speaker so I could work and listen at the same time — multi-tasking as usual. I heard our associate director's voice, usually so friendly and upbeat, take on a somber tone. He stuttered and stumbled, which was not like him, and finally gave us the bad news.

"You are all being relocated to Ohio, if you are willing to move," he told us with a tremble in his voice, "and if you cannot move, you will be given a severance package, and sixty days notice."

I felt numb. How could this be happening? Most of us had been at the company for years and had been told our jobs were some of the most secure in the organization. None of us, for various reasons, would be able to relocate, and there were no other jobs available within the company in our area, so it appeared my team and I would soon be out of work.

I had the heartbreaking task of sharing the news with my staff. As their leader, I had to be strong, upbeat, and courageous, but inside I was scared to death. While I gave them words of encouragement, I felt my world was slowly coming to an end.

My husband and family consoled me, but I was scared. Really scared. Financially, I knew we would be okay — my husband had a good job, and the severance and other savings I had would keep us going for quite a while, but I had worked full-time my whole life and did not know if I could deal with losing my job. It had become my identity — who I was and how I defined myself. I was a leader, and I felt, a good one. What would I be with that taken from me?

The first few days after my job ended, I

didn't want to get out of bed. I kept up a brave front for my children and husband, but moped around the house, not really knowing what to do. After working nonstop for twenty-five years I was lost. I sent out résumés, but due to the economic conditions, job postings in my field were few and far between. It looked like I would be out of work for quite awhile, and I didn't know what to do with all my newfound extra time.

One day, after sitting around feeling sorry for myself, I turned on the television and watched a program about a missions group that helped children and hungry people all over the world. I felt guilty knowing that even though I had lost my job, we had plenty of good, healthy food on the table every night. The words spoken by the missionary seemed directed specifically at me — she told viewers that the "best way to be blessed and to forget about your own problems is to help someone else."

Ashamed, I realized that I had been wallowing in self-pity when I had so much to be thankful for — a loving husband, beautiful children, and family and friends who needed me. I could either continue to focus on what I had lost and be miserable, or I could count my blessings and bless others.

I decided to get up, get dressed, and cook a great meal for my family that night. I had always loved to cook, learning at the side of my mom and grandmothers, all wonderful Southern cooks who taught me their secrets. I also thought I could make some extra food to take to our neighbors who were retired, and brighten their day as well.

I began to assemble the ingredients for my dinner, humming to myself a little as I prepared our meal. I was starting to feel like my old self again. Just then one of my daughters walked into the kitchen and asked if she could help me cook dinner. As we stirred and sifted, basted and baked, our dinner came together. We laughed, talked, and shared stories. I told her how my mom and grandmothers had let me help them cook when I was a little girl, and I still used many of their recipes. I forgot about how depressed I had been, and when we put the meal on the table for the rest of the family, we were both proud of the delicious dinner we had made and basked in the compliments we received.

After dinner, as I cleaned up the dishes, it occurred to me that I had never taught my children to cook. I had been so busy being a "career woman" that I had not taken the time to show them how to make the wonderful dishes I had learned to make as a child and young woman. I had always cooked for my family, but had not given them the gift that I had been given — the gift of learning how to prepare a meal for my loved ones. I was saddened by this, and decided that I was going to use my unexpected free time to change all that.

The next morning I announced to my family that I was going to start a cooking school for them. This was met with groans from my kids, who all had busy lives and plans of their own. But I convinced them to give it a try and we decided we would prepare supper the next night. I let each child pick a dish to prepare for the meal, with my guidance. We decided to do this weekly and make extra food to share with friends or neighbors in need in our community.

The next morning, we shopped for our dinner at our grocery store and local farmers market. We unloaded our ingredients, put on our aprons, and started cooking. I shared cooking techniques, short cuts, and the background behind many of the recipes we had decided to prepare. While making my grandmother's famous lemon meringue pie, I remembered the many times I had stood in her kitchen, licking the beaters thick with white, fluffy meringue, sweet and cloudlike, and how much fun those times had been. Now I was sharing them with my own children. I could almost see Grandmother smiling down from heaven, watching my children and I carrying on her traditions. Nothing had made her happier than cooking something wonderful for her family, and now I knew how she felt. Instead of rushing to put something quick on the table between business meetings and reports, I got to take the time to enjoy cooking and eating the beautiful meal we were creating. Plus, I got to share the company of my children — listen to them joke, find out what was going on with each of them, and appreciate the personalities of each one. All four of them were so different, yet so special, and brought so much joy into my life — I had just been too busy to notice that before. I had been so busy providing for my family financially, and basing my worth on my career, that I had forgotten what was really worthwhile, and who I really was — a wife and a mother to these amazing people who deserved my time, my guidance, and affection.

Cooking school continued each week. It became a time we all looked forward to — a time of laughter, love and learning. And, of course, some really great meals. Cooking with my kids was just the start — I began doing

things with them and for them that they
enjoyed — going to the library, movies, playing tennis, or lounging by the pool. For the first
time, I was able to really focus on and enjoy
my family, without deadlines looming in the
background, working on my laptop, or check-
ing my e-mail at the same time. Instead of
multi-tasking, I focused on the one task that
mattered most — making sure my family
knew that they were loved and were number
one in my life.

I did eventually go back to work, but I
found a job that was more flexible and allowed
me to spend much more time with my husband and children. It turned out to be an even
better job than my previous one — it paid better, was much less stressful, and gave me the
flexibility I needed to be there when my family
needed me. My priorities had changed, and I
never again wanted to put my loved ones in
second place to my career.

I had thought losing my job was the worst
thing that had ever happened to me. But, it

turned out to be a blessing in disguise. While I had thought that losing my job was the end of who I was, it was really only the beginning of discovering the real me.

~Melanie Adams Hardy

Walking Through My Paralysis

It has taken me seven years to consciously relive the events of January 22nd, 2003. It's not that I've developed courage to face what happened. I relive it in my dreams. Many nights my husband, Bob, wakes me because I'm screaming. I should have stopped repressing the memories years ago. It is time to tell my story.

Many concerned people have asked me the specifics of what happened, yet apologize for prying. Nobody's prying. It has been my fear of facing as well as telling the truth. As Christopher Reeve said, "Living in fear is not living at all."

Cape Cod, where I live, is a kayaker's dream. For years, Bob and I were four-season kayakers. We planned our work schedules around the tides. Two days before my breakdown, Bob and I had taken a beautiful winter excursion in Cape Cod Bay, where curious harbor seals escorted our boat.

That night, weird symptoms began. In bed, I couldn't keep my legs still. Until dawn, I sat watching TV while continuously needing to swing my legs back and forth.

The next night it became hellish. I needed to stand up and sit down constantly. Then it felt like electrical impulses gone haywire. My legs, seemingly on their own, were flinging up as far as legs could go. I couldn't stop them.

Bob called our friend, Judy, who's a chief doctor at a Boston hospital about two hours from our home. I could tell Bob was trying to control his panic.

"What did she say?" I said.

"It's not good."

"Just tell me!"

"She said, 'Take Saralee to my hospital's emergency room right now. I'll meet you there.'"

"What does she think is wrong?"

"She thinks it's your spinal cord."

I was shocked. "I didn't have an accident! And I don't have pain!"

"I told her that. But she said, 'Something's happening very fast.'"

When I was wheeled into the hospital, I couldn't walk and had no feeling in my hands. I was petrified.

Three neurologists tested me. I looked away as they touched sharp instruments to my body. I felt nothing. Bob saw the startling abnormalities. For my sake, he never showed his terror on his face.

A CAT scan ruled out a brain tumor. Nearly everything was ruled out: multiple sclerosis, bone disease, rheumatoid arthritis.

I needed an MRI but their machine was down. Now I had no feeling in my legs and arms. Since I was losing precious function so fast, we decided to go to another hospital.

A neurologist rushed to stop us. "If you leave here," he said, "you could become a quadriplegic and permanently on a vent." So of course we stayed.

By the time of my MRI, I had no feeling in my torso.

The chief neurologist of several Boston hospitals had been called in. My medical team observed as we looked at my MRI images.

Two vertebrae in my neck had completely disengaged and were rapidly crossing over each other, choking off my spinal cord. Without immediate surgery, the cord would be severed entirely and I'd be completely paralyzed.

Why did this happen? Nobody knew.

It happened spontaneously.

"Can you fix it?"

"No." He was a straight shooter. "What's done is done. We can hopefully stop the progression surgically."

"Hopefully?"

"There's no guarantee of improvement.

There's a fifty percent chance that even with surgery you will never walk again."

I slung my arms over the ledge of the nurses' station. I was in an advanced state of spasticity. Everything was moving on its own. My arms and legs were uncontrollably swinging widely through the air. "Are you telling me that even if surgery stopped the progression, I could spend the rest of my life like this?"

"Yes."

The surgery did stop the progression.

My neurologist said, "If there's any improvement, ninety percent will occur in the first three days. The only other variable that could help is time. Whatever state your body is in two years from now, you will always be."

Bob asked if occupational therapy, physical therapy, or medication would help. He shook his head no. My doctor's words felt as authoritative as an edict from God.

I'd rather not name my doctors. They did terrific surgery. I love them all and we get along beautifully. However I'm disappointed in myself that I initially took their words as gospel. Christopher Reeve didn't listen to his doctors. He said, "It's pretty irrefutable that you can help yourself. I just don't believe in ultimatums."

I wish I had been prepared for the psychological and physiological aftereffects. Bob was angry. "They sent you into a whole new world without telling you one thing to expect."

There was no improvement in those three days.

I kept falling. My brain was sending incorrect signals, such as how high to lift my foot over a two-inch obstacle. Had the medical professionals told me two words — "look down" — many dangerous falls would never have happened.

Christopher Reeve said, "Gratitude, like love, needs to be active." When I regained use of my typing fingers, I started using them with gusto.

I'm privileged to help others by writing for the Christopher and Dana Reeve Foundation, though I'm still surprised every time I see myself described on their website as a "woman living with paralysis." Paralysis is defined by the foundation as a central nervous system disorder resulting in difficulty or inability to move the upper or lower extremities. As Christopher said, "Living a life with meaning means spreading the word. Even if you can't move, you can have a powerful effect with what you say." Using my writing to help other people with disabilities has become a mission for me. After all, Christopher also said, "Even if your body doesn't work the way it used to, the heart and the mind and the spirit are not diminished."

In these seven years, I haven't been able to change some malfunctions … yet. Walking feels like I'm on a tightrope while moving through molasses. Though I can walk, I can't climb one step. With no balance, I can't stand still. But I've become determined to help myself. Again I take inspiration from Christopher Reeve, who said, "I gradually stopped wondering, 'What life do I have?' and began to consider, 'What life can I build?'"

I learned that there's no greater antidepressant than helping others. It is dramatically gratifying to make a difference in others' lives through my writing. The countless readers' responses I receive have without a doubt brought meaning to what happened in 2003. I am eternally grateful for all who have helped me by telling me my words are important to them.

My wish is that those who read this story might re-think the words "try" and "hope."

Before my spinal cord collapse, I spent nearly every day kayaking in the magical world of Cape Cod Bay. I assumed those days were gone for good, but now I know they are not. Bob and I have taken five small excursions back to the bay. The curious seals are still there, probably wondering where we've been all these years. I tell them, from my strongest heart and resounding voice, what Christopher Reeve said: "I refuse to allow a disability to determine how I live my life. There is only one way to go in life and that is forward."

At that two-year mark, which is when my neurologist said that whatever I was, I would always be, I could walk no further than twenty feet. This year, which is seven years later, I made it ten miles.

~Saralee Perel

The Gift of Brain Cancer

In August 2002, I received the greatest gift of my life when I was told that I had terminal brain cancer and would be dead in four to six months. I had been married exactly five months when this happened. My career was going well, my family and friends loved me. I was as happy as I had ever been. So why was this such a great gift? Why?

Because I had to face my death.

It was the middle of the night in January 2003. I was wandering outside in the cold, alone and bitter. The clinical trial I had entered was fraught with uncertainty and danger. I could only participate because I was terminal, my survival quite unlikely. I was confused, constantly nauseous, and hardly able to walk, even with a cane.

I was infuriated by my circumstances: I hated the cancer, myself, the doctors, and God. I found myself shouting, screaming, crying, raging against the injustice. For the first time in fifty-four years I had finally found happiness in my life, and now this horrific disease was ripping from me not only the joy of life, but also any semblance of stability, comfort or peace. Was I destined for continuous detestable rotting away every day in my pathetic limp to a cold grave?

Then suddenly, amidst all the virulence, came the inspirational voice of a very dear old friend, employer, and mentor, W. Clement Stone, one of the first people to write about Positive Mental Attitude, or PMA. In my mind I could hear him say, as he had thousands of times, "Every Adversity carries within it the seed of equivalent or greater benefit to those who have a Positive Mental Attitude!"

What?

Are you serious?

Greater Benefit?

What on earth was the greater benefit of dying of brain cancer, old man? (I was unaware that Mr. Stone had passed away just five months earlier at the age of 100.)

His words kept running through the part of my brain that was still functioning. Not some adversity, he had said, but every adversity, EVERY adversity, carries within it that seed of equivalent or greater benefit! You have to be kidding!

Fortunately, the many years of his being my mentor, teacher and hero had left its mark — the words "I reasoned" were ablaze like sun above my head. He used "I reasoned" frequently — very often in describing critical situations he faced in life. Once, a loaded gun was held to his head by a desperate, depressed, and hopeless person who told him that he had lost everything — he was going to kill Mr. Stone, and then turn the gun on himself. While most of us would panic in such a spot, Mr. Stone said calmly, "I reasoned," and then proceeded to think of a logical plan to save not only himself but the other person as well. He later set the person up in business, where the man was successful and prosperous the rest of his life.

"So," I said to myself, giving in to his message, "Let's reason." Immediately, I was at peace and felt rational — for the first time in months.

So ... what were the possibilities for me? After all, life at that point had not provided me with very good options.

I certainly didn't have the option of "live happily ever after" — or did I?

The fact is one of two things was going to happen: I was either going to die very shortly, or, much less likely, live a long time.

So what if I died soon?

Well, "I reasoned," if I were bitter and angry, then I would have spent the last few months of my life in sorrow and isolation, making a living hell for my loved ones, and would be remembered, if at all, as a bitter old man who let brain cancer defeat him. I would receive their temporary show of sympathy, but in the end they would only have contempt for me and how I left them.

On the other hand, what if I were positive and hopeful? It wouldn't change the date of my death one bit!

But, it would mean that I would spend the last months of my life breathing deeply and clearly, contented, blissful, and in love with my family and everyone I met. I would die a happy man, and be remembered as that brave soul who faced a terrible death with courage, fortitude and aplomb. I would be cherished by those who knew me.

On the other hand, what if I made it? What if I lived?

Then I had no reason to be bitter and tormented! Why waste months of my life wailing about an end that wasn't even near?

So there it was — I had every reason to be positive about my condition, and absolutely no reason to be negative.

It was at that point, that very moment in

time, for the first time in my life, that I stopped dying and started living.

I started telling everyone I met and knew that having brain cancer was the greatest thing that had ever happened to me, and today I believe that with all my heart.

A little over a year ago, I learned that the brain cancer had returned. Treatment today is more researched and predictable, prognosis is better; however, the outcome is never certain. After a year of radiation and chemotherapy the tumor board doctors have decided to continue my chemotherapy indefinitely and have scheduled me for monthly MRIs, with absolutely no promises.

How has this disturbing news affected me? It has made me even more positive!

From that special moment — that cold, dark night in January 2003, I have not wasted one second of my life fretting about dying. All the moments of all of my days are spent living.

Brain cancer the first time made me a better man. The second time is making me a good man. Brain cancer is the greatest thing that has ever happened to me.

So what about you? You will have good things and bad in life. Sometimes life will give you great fortune, other times it will rip you like a brick across the face.

What happens to you will happen, and you only have two ways to respond — you can be positive and happy, or negative and miserable. That's it. The good news is that the choice is always up to you! You choose how happy you will be every day of your life, every way that life happens, no matter when, no matter what, no matter who.

Make the decision today to live, not die. To be positive, not negative. Don't endure a tragedy such as mine to figure it out. Live every day, live every minute, live every second of your life.

~Tom Schumm

She Altered My Attitude

My ninety-year-old grandmother rested quietly in her hospital bed after a visit from her heart surgeon. He explained that she needed a quadruple bypass and she clung to the only good news he delivered: she had the body of a seventy-year-old.

Grandma's vanity required that she still dye her hair and the brown curls framed her porcelain face, her warm eyes, and her thin-lipped smile as she asked, "What would you do?"

My grandfather had died nearly thirty years earlier and Grandma had independently made decisions ever since. I knew she'd made up her mind before she'd even asked, but she liked me to feel included in her life especially after my mother passed away.

"I'd have the surgery," I said.

She nodded and then softly said, "I don't want to go home and wait to die. Besides, I'll be fine."

She was right. A few days later, a post-op nurse allowed me to visit Grandma in the recovery room after her surgery, a rather unusual privilege in hindsight. I was relieved Grandma had survived the operation but had been strangely confident that she would. Surprisingly, she lay naked and unconscious on the gurney, not yet cleaned up or bandaged. She had yellow iodine smeared all over her upper body between her elongated breasts and I was impressed that her enormous incision was stitched together as perfectly as any seam she'd ever sewn.

The sight of her chest rising and falling was comforting, but if Grandma had been awake she would have been embarrassed for me to see her naked. I held her hand and pondered the point at which my body would look like her medically speaking "seventy-year-old" one and worried that given my stressful job, it would be by the time I was forty instead of ninety.

About a year after my Grandma's successful surgery, my partner Ann and I invited her to our house for barbecued ribs. It was one of her favorite meals. I thought she'd enjoy a diversion from the usual mashed potatoes and gravy fare served daily at her assisted living apartment.

That particular Thursday night, both Ann and I got stuck at work. We got home only minutes before Grandma arrived, which killed any hope of serving her normal early dinner. I bought some time by offering to show her my nearby office while Ann got dinner going.

I helped Grandma carefully lower herself into my sports car and then I drove the short distance to my company's headquarters. She almost gasped as I turned down the tree-lined driveway that framed the roadway to the front of the building. Her face was full of wonder, like it always was, and her bright eyes took in everything around her.

"It's so beautiful," she said. "It looks like a park."

I'd never really thought of the grounds that way. My mind was usually distracted by the latest project delay or staff crisis. I drove to the private driveway at the back of the building and used my security card to enter the underground garage. The automatic door slowly opened and I parked my car in my assigned spot and started her tour.

Grandma was impressed with everything: the pristine underground garage, the sheer number of cubicles that stretched as far as the eye could see, the variety of logo-wear for sale at the company store, and the smell of food wafting from the full-service dining room.

As we stepped into the cafeteria I asked, "Given your diabetes, should we grab something here to hold you over until we get home?"

She looked at the herbed chicken dinner,

the salad, soup, and sandwich bars and said, "I don't want to spoil my appetite, but do they serve such extravagant meals every night?"

Again, through her eyes I'd taken the quality and convenience of our cafeteria for granted, but the aromas made me want to head home for our own dinner.

"Just one more stop on the tour, Grandma. I want to show you where I sit."

We walked to my office and we both plopped down in chairs around my small conference table. She stroked the mahogany and said, "This is really nice." Then she pointed across my office to the chair behind my desk and asked, "Who sits there?"

Grandmother had always gotten a glazed look on her face whenever I explained what I did for a living, but it seemed she thought I worked at the conference table while "my boss" sat in the big chair behind the desk. Knowing she had been impressed with even that, I giggled as I said, "Well, Grandma... I do... this entire office is mine. I usually sit there at the computer and use this table for meetings with my staff."

Her eyes flashed with astonishment and she looked around my office with a new appreciation. Her response struck me. She'd attended teacher's college — or normal school as she called it — but when she got pregnant with my father she gave up her career. The opportunities for women had expanded far beyond those available to my grandmother: teacher, nurse, secretary, or homemaker.

She went over and sat down in my desk chair. She spun the chair around and then, one by one, she stared at the photographs of Canyonlands, Zion, and Yosemite National Parks that I'd taken while on vacations.

I pointed to one picture on the wall entitled "Attitude." It had a rainbow stretched above a roaring mountain stream and William James' words embossed at the bottom.

"I bought it with your Christmas money last year."

She looked at the picture, drew in a deep

breath and then read the words out loud, "The greatest discovery of any generation is that a human being can alter his life by altering his attitudes."

She said, "I like all your pictures, but I think that one's my favorite."

"Me too, Grandma. Are you ready to go home and eat?"

She nodded. As we left my office she stopped outside the door and looked back. She gestured towards my nameplate and said, "I didn't notice that when we walked in."

She touched the letters of my last name... of her last name... and then she looped her arm through mine, patted my wrist, and said, "You've certainly done very well for yourself. I'm so proud of you."

When we got back to my house, Grandma patiently waited for us to serve dinner. It was almost eight when we finally sat down for our meal. Grandma attempted to eat her plate of ribs, but the pork was tough as bricks. When she finished eating what she could, she wiped her mouth with her napkin and unwittingly summed up her philosophy of life: "That barbecue sauce sure was tasty!"

My employer's headquarters, my office, and even my job never looked as wonderful as they did, that day, through my grandmother's eyes — her glistening grey eyes that always sparkled with possibility and only lingered on the good, especially when she looked at me.

~Kris Flaa

Getting Old Gratefully

When I turned sixty-eight, old age seemed to have arrived. Seventy loomed close, and felt especially ominous, as my mother died at seventy-two. My husband Tom, ever the optimist, reminded me that my father lived to be ninety-four — also, that I'm a lot more active and health-conscious than my mother was. After all, we stretch every morning before a breakfast of steel-cut oatmeal, take our vitamins and supplements, get plenty of exercise, and have meaningful days. Mine are filled with gardening and writing, Tom's with singing, playing keyboard and trumpet.

Still, sometimes it takes two of us to come up with an acquaintance's name, or the title of a movie we saw just yesterday! Once I could garden nonstop for six hours, but now I need a break after two hours. Then there are those startling moments when I turn the corner in a store to face an unexpected mirror. Who is that old person in the glass?

It's no accident that the three light bulbs above the mirror in my bathroom are now fifteen watts. I like that soft glow. Besides, without my reading glasses I can't see the wrinkles, although it does seem that my eyes are shrinking. Is it time for an eyelift? In a heartbeat, dread of surgery overcomes vanity. Then I think to myself that I've simply got to find a way to accept old age with all its changes. I'm making the last years of my life miserable with worry!

When I started to worry about aging, I decided to get some help from my friends in the Golden Years Gardening Group. We meet once a month to talk about our gardens and anything else on our minds. We're all women over sixty with a common love for plants. I proposed that our next meeting topic be "The

Positive Aspects of Aging."

I worried that no one would show up. Why on earth had I suggested this topic? It might be too serious, too fraught with anxiety. So what a relief that most everyone showed up.

Gail Austin started the Golden Years Gardening Group a year after her husband Ken died. She wanted more time to spend with friends, to enjoy life — to work less and play more. As she began simplifying her large, high-maintenance garden, Gail realized that many older gardeners were struggling with a similar process and could use a support group to help them accept life's changing circumstances. We would share the adventure of letting go of stressful work and learn to enjoy less complicated gardens.

That afternoon Gail suggested we go around the room and give each person her turn to speak about the benefits of aging, without any interruptions. She began with a key statement.

"I don't worry about the little things anymore," Gail said. "Forty was the beginning."

This theme — the perspective we gain after experiencing many of life's changes over time — came up repeatedly. Hazel, a recent member, put a similar idea in her own words.

"Resilience," she said. "Life experience has given me that." There was a moment of quiet in the room as we all absorbed the importance of Hazel's wisdom. By now, some of us were nodding our heads in agreement, smiling in recognition of this big advantage of growing old.

Next, Lisa announced another common thread.

"My grandchild," she said. "I understand now why my grandmother meant a lot to me. I understand the love she was giving to me and can transmit it to my granddaughter." Some of Lisa's grandmother's love came in the form of discipline. Now Lisa practices that same tough love with her granddaughter, helping her set boundaries.

Jepi added another layer to the topic of

family connections.

"I have a new relationship with my dad, who's eighty-nine," she said. "He became a gardener in his late seventies." Now they share that passion and spend time together in the garden. Her dad is slow, but that's just fine. What's important is that they're growing closer.

Dru reminded us about the importance of a positive attitude.

"I'm a 'cup is half full' kind of person, not a 'cup is half empty,' and I'm lucky for that," she said.

Ann echoed Dru's affirmation, adding more details.

"The cup is full, a new day is always wonderful. I feel appreciation to be here," she said. Ann practices gratitude each evening, reviewing the gifts of the day before she goes to sleep.

Diane reminded us about financial independence.

"I feel lucky to have retirement income," she said. "Now it's fun to get up at 6 AM!"

Renee piggybacked on that idea:

"I finally have my independence," she said. "I get to decide what I want to do."

By this time, I was feeling pretty good about growing old. I hadn't prepared what I'd say, but when my turn came I knew just what it was. Without any rehearsing, I blurted it out.

"I'm so happy to have found love late in life," I said. "I met Tom when I was fifty-eight years old, and we married five years later. After twenty-three years of being divorced, falling in love with a wonderful man was a great gift of older age."

I put my arm around Diana, who sat next to me in the circle of friends. We'd been gardening friends for many years, way before Golden Gardeners had been formed.

"Diana here was my role model — she encouraged me not to give up, to keep searching until I found the right man," I said.

Diana smiled and explained to the group that it took her five marriages before she found a lasting love. Both of us married younger men who would have been out of the picture when we were in our twenties — actually they would have been in high school! As we get older, ten years difference in age doesn't matter.

I thought more about how getting older helps us love more deeply. Tom is there for me when I'm sick, just as much as when I'm healthy. A natural-born comedian, he keeps me laughing every day, the best tonic I know. When I was younger, I never would have considered a short, bald man who'd been married and divorced three times. But when I met Tom, all I could see was his beautiful smile, warm blue eyes, and loving heart. I gave him extra credit for continuing to marry; I'd met so many men who'd become embittered after even one divorce. Tom's hopefulness gave me courage to marry again.

Our group had helped me more than I'd imagined. Not only were my worries about growing older quieting down — I was actually thrilled to be in this stage of life, now that I saw the big picture. Best of all, our circle had grown closer after sharing these intimate details of our lives. I looked around at my friends with greater understanding, respect and love. How wonderful to be part of this gathering of wise women, all of us lending strength to each other on such an interesting journey.

~Barbara Blossom Ashmun

World Travel with Asperger's

London, England, Late April 1998: My first full day in a foreign country. It was the first of many Western European countries I'd visit on my group tour. I ventured out a few blocks from my hotel and came upon an Underground (subway) station that could take me virtually anywhere in the metropolitan area. How I wanted to go to Parliament to watch the House of Commons debate! I approached the Underground entrance, but then I suddenly froze: the steps that most people would simply descend in order to get from Point A to Point B were for me synonymous with being confronted with a million things to juggle simultaneously.

A condition that I live with every day made

it almost impossible for me to satisfy my desire. It's a neurobiological disorder called Asperger's syndrome. Those who have this condition experience a wide range of symptoms and behaviors, like taking in every little bit of stimuli that their surroundings emanate. So when an environment isn't familiar, it can be too overwhelming to handle, which is what I was experiencing at that moment.

I struggle with my condition but I have learned to overcome it in order to pursue my passion for world travel.

I went on that group tour thinking the itinerary would fill my time with all the sightseeing and exploring I could ever hope for, along with the security of traveling with others. I quickly discovered this wasn't the case. Free time for exploring on our own was often scheduled for the group. As a result of my condition, I restricted myself to exploring only those areas that were within walking distance of my hotel, which made me feel very cheated: London was beckoning and here I was clinging to sites around Hyde Park!

My first trip abroad progressed southward over the next few weeks all the way to Athens, Greece. My poor sense of direction, also inherent in my condition, almost got me into dire straits on more than one occasion. As with London, I was only blocks away from my hotels in the cities of Brussels, Belgium, and Innsbruck, Austria. Yet I found myself wandering aimlessly through the night in those two cities, asking myself how I would find my way back to the hotels where my tour group was staying. Only with the help of the police and/or very conspicuous landmarks did I manage to return to the hotels... eventually. On rare occasions, I would hang out with one or two people in the tour group during our free time to do some off-the-beaten-path exploring. I relied on them to get us where we needed to be, and thus my sense of inadequacy was only heightened.

When I got back to the USA, I knew that something was going to have to change. I knew deep down that my love for traveling and exploring was stronger than the handicaps of my condition. For almost a year and a half, the debacles of my first foreign trip would haunt me. By the autumn of 1999, I felt compelled to go back to London, vowing to travel independently on the subways and buses to all the parts of the great city no matter how scary that seemed, no matter how lost I would get.

I knew that for me to become the independent traveler that I wished in my soul to be, I would have to compensate for my natural shortcomings with two things. First, I would have to study extra hard the detailed maps provided by tourism departments and the Internet before embarking, using positive visualization of finding my way around. Second, once abroad, I needed to acquire the gumption to go up to complete strangers to ask them if I was on the right path to one of London's icons even if that meant doing so every other block along the way. This would keep my sense of direction in check. For many people with

Asperger's syndrome, going up to the locals to interact is also a challenge, as we are not generally the most sociable folks in the population. The bottom line was that in order for my aspirations to be realized, I had to seize my Asperger's syndrome by the horns.

My friend from Virginia would accompany me for the first part of the trip. We'd be together, but I'd act like I was alone while trying to figure out how to get to a certain destination. He'd only interject if I began to take a wrong turn. This technique proved to be very effective. He headed back to the States a few days before me, but I survived being totally alone in the metropolis. Consequentially, I developed a new confidence in trekking the world independently.

A year later, in October of 2000, it was I who would play tour guide, so to speak, as I took another friend of mine all over London and its surrounding areas. Sometimes, my sense of direction resulted in some minor inconveniences for us, but I persevered. The end result was a trip full of sightseeing successes!

Since that first fateful trip abroad in '98, where I let my disability diminish my sense of adventure, I have taken even more trips to Western Europe, China, South Africa, and Panama, mostly on my own. I've secured hotel reservations, train and bus tickets, etc., all over the world. I've challenged myself even further via my journeys to Spain, Panama, and Italy. I had to be even more resourceful while visiting these countries, given that I am not fluent in Spanish or Italian. I got around fine with the aid of really detailed and user-friendly phrase books. The locals in those countries appreciated my attempts at using their language to communicate with them.

By 2004, I had enough travel experiences to feel confident in submitting travel articles to various publications. I've now had many of them published in various magazines and online sites for pay. Globe-trotting inspired me to confront my Asperger's syndrome in a way that I wouldn't have done otherwise, and ultimately led me to a new career as a travel writer.

When I look back at my initial reactions on that 1998 London trip, I am amazed at the changes and the consistencies. The difficulties remain, but now I know I can deal with them and I have a backlog of memories and techniques for dealing with my disability. I may still feel hesitant about putting myself into a situation where I'm unfamiliar with the environment and feeling overwhelmed with the sensory overload, but I also know I can control my reaction and draw on my past experiences to get through the moment in order to fulfill my desires.

The key to overcoming obstacles is having a desire that is stronger than the reality of the obstacles. It is that inner quest which will lead one to find ways of overcoming!

~Roy A. Barnes

I Can Get Through This

Sprawled across the front seat of my car, I taste it. Blood. A mouthful of it. Suddenly, someone taps on my shattered driver-side window. "Miss, can you hear me?"

I try to respond, but I can't seem to make myself do so.

"No, no, don't move. We're coming in to get you."

I finally put it together that my Good Samaritan is a police officer, and that I've been involved in an accident. My rescuers are now trying to cut me out of the car, the rear of which is smashed into the front, rendering the doors inoperable and the backseat destroyed. "Wait," I cry, panicked. "Where are my sons?"

The officer appears confused, and that's

when I remember: I'd been on my way to work and had just left my two young sons with our babysitter. Relief pours through me as I relate this now to the officer. "What a blessing," he says. "If they'd been in the backseat, they'd be gone."

His observation is sobering, and I panic anew.

"Hey now, you're okay, and so are your boys. You can get through this."

I nod, managing to thank him, even though my face feels so crooked I can barely speak. As I'm loaded into the ambulance, I notice that it's the kind of day to rejoice in, a beautiful blue Indian summer day with Thanksgiving a mere week away, and I offer my own tearful prayer of thanksgiving. I'm so grateful to be safe, and so much more, to know that my boys are safe.

What I can't know in that moment, however, is just how long my injuries will affect me. In the first years after the accident, I undergo extensive dental work, a bone graft to my fractured maxilla, and some sixteen root canals and implants to repair my damaged teeth. I begin suffering sometimes agonizing face, neck, and ear pain, and my mouth opening starts to decrease, making dental work hard to accomplish. It disrupts the "little" things too — eating, kissing, brushing and flossing, even talking. My oral surgeon suspects temporomandibular joint disorder in my jaw joints, and MRIs and a painful procedure called an arthrogram confirm his diagnosis.

The temporomandibular joint is that little unassuming bump in front of each ear that joins the lower jaw to the temporal bone of the skull. It's a complex joint in that it enables the mouth to move both up and down and from side to side. A normal mouth can open to forty-five millimeters; mine gets down to four at one point. My doctors try to stabilize things with splints and non-invasive "stretching" procedures, but finally, five years after the accident, my surgeon performs two open-joint surgeries, which, unfortunately, provide nominal relief. I continue to struggle with eating and a limited opening. Liquids and soft foods are all I can manage, and to "crank" my mouth open, my doctor tries an apparatus that resembles a hefty eyelash curler. But even this I can't accommodate, so he resorts to tongue depressors, forcing one flat stick into my mouth atop the other. This keeps the joints moving and breaks scar tissue, but the pain it causes nearly lifts me out of my chair. "One tongue depressor at a time, Theresa," he encourages me, wiping away my tears. "You can get through this."

I nod, conveying my thanks with my eyes.

Eighteen years after the accident, my jaw has deteriorated to such a point that the joint bones have fused, leaving virtually no movement. Heat pads, ice packs, and medication have become constant companions, and the pain often sends me to bed. It takes a toll on my work and family, and it's increasingly hard to think positive. My doctor believes that the only thing left for me is total joint replacement, a very specialized undertaking. Of course, I worry. How pervasive will my scars be? With such a limited opening, can I even be intubated safely? But I have every confidence in my new surgeon. In a thirteen-plus-hour procedure, I am fitted with prosthetics made of titanium and screwed into bone. After surgery, my mouth is wired shut for three long months and I must learn to eat through syringes. I "shoot" Ensure and other liquids into the tight open space between my cheek and clamped teeth, dreaming of a day when I might chew.

When bandages are removed, I get a first good look at my face, and I tremble in awe when I see it. For so long, I'd feared this would end badly, but thanks to my surgeon's artist's hands, my scars, once healed, will be minimal and mostly hidden in my neck and hairline. One complication arises, however: I can't close my eyes. This is due to nerve damage, and it makes for a blurry, no-blinking world. By day, I can scarcely see, and by night, I tape my eyelids shut to sleep. With my mouth that can't open and my eyes that won't close, I feel trapped inside my body, wondering if I'll ever truly be "me." To rejuvenate the nerves, I use a daunting device that my husband lovingly calls "the stun gun," and slowly, with this electrical stimulation, the muscle movement around my eyes returns. After the wires come off, I embark on nearly two years of physical therapy with a therapist who must manually manipulate my jaw. He is gentle and strong in equal measures, and, knowing I can get through this, I vow to follow his lead.

Today, twenty-seven years after my accident, I keep in mind just how much I've been blessed. I've doctors who still greet me with hugs, family and friends who have been with me every step of my journey. The accident and its aftermath have taught me that with a little faith and a lot of determination, I can get through anything. Yes, I still live with chronic pain, and I know that because the prosthetics degrade over time, I will face at least one more replacement surgery in the future. But it's also because of that surgery that I've now achieved real quality of life. I may not be able to eat salad or meat or popcorn at the movies, but I can still go to the movies. I may use baby toothbrushes and sleep propped with pillows and heat pads, but I can still wake to welcome the dawn. And yes, I worry that all the surgeries, all the years of medication and less than optimal diet could shorten my lifespan, but I've learned that life is meant to be lived a moment at a time. For we are not, praise God, like jigsaw puzzles. Our pieces don't necessarily have to be interlocking and uniformly cut for us to feel complete. I look in the mirror and I say to myself: this is what I have; this is who I am. I am strong, and I am here. And no matter what difficulties life might bring, I know I've stared fear straight in the eye before and I can do it again, emerging proud and shining.

~Theresa Sanders

Moving Forward

Our old neighborhood had been like modern-day Mayberry. Neighbors chatted over fences. Newcomers were welcomed with chocolate brownies and butter-braid bread. It had been easy to find friends there.

Our new community was different. It seemed that family roots grew deep. Deep as the Mississippi River that flowed past the tiny river town. Breaking in was tough.

We'd moved to decrease my husband's commute to work. Only thirty miles.

I wished that I could erase each one.

After living there for six months, I was ready to pick up tent stakes and move back home. I was lonely for a friend. My three boys were lonely. My husband, Lonny, fared okay, but he spent his days at work.

"I'm so alone here," I said to Lonny one evening. "I don't see my old friends much, and I can't seem to make new ones." We were sitting on the front porch of our old Victorian. Our three young sons kicked a soccer ball around the side yard.

Lonny is a good listener, but he also has an engineer's brain. He's a problem solver. "What have you done to meet people?" he asked.

"I go to story time at the library every week. I initiate conversations at the park. I even stalked a lady at a garage sale. She had two boys and looked like someone I'd want to be friends with. But she was more interested in that old vase she was looking at than chatting."

"Sounds like you're doing the right stuff," he said. "Keep at it."

And I did. I tried to be open and friendly. It wasn't that people were unkind. They just all seemed established.

A few more months passed and winter settled in. It was harder than ever to meet people. I admitted that we had a few obstacles. We homeschooled our boys and still attended church in our old community. But I'd never had trouble making friends before, and I started to develop an attitude. Who needed a friend? I was tired of trying to fit in a place it seemed that we didn't belong.

Grey winter days eventually gave way to fresh spring color, but my attitude stayed dark and gloomy. I began to feel bitter. I still went to the library and park, but I didn't start conversations. I didn't invite anyone over. I wanted to move back to our old neighborhood.

Lonny noticed my sinking disposition.

"Shawnelle, you look unapproachable," he whispered in my ear one afternoon. He and I were sitting in lawn chairs at our son's first-of-the-season Little League game. Samuel, our three-year-old watched the game from his own little Scooby-Doo chair.

"What do you mean?"

"Body language. Your arms are crossed. You placed our chairs fifteen yards away from everyone else."

"It doesn't matter. I'm not going to have friends here."

"You sure won't if you stop trying," he said.

Just then Samuel looked up. He must've heard our whispers. "Mom's right, Dad. We'll never ever have friends here. And we just want to go home."

I sat there and looked at my tiny blond son.

His words mirrored my attitude. And I didn't like the murky reflection. That's when I knew that I needed an adjustment. I didn't want my boys to learn that the way to work through a tough time was to wield a wounded and bitter attitude.

Over the next few months I worked very hard. I smiled when I didn't feel like it. I joined conversations at the ballpark. The boys and I baked cookies for our neighbors. It's going to be great when I find that friend, I told myself. I'll appreciate it even more than if I'd made friends right away. I stopped talking about moving back home. We signed up for reading programs at the library and frequented parks and the bike path along the river. I was still lonely, but some of the frustration slipped away. At least I wasn't sitting home stewing. And it was harder to grumble when I was smiling.

I went forward each day. Doing the things I could do. Trying not to look back.

One afternoon Samuel and I clambered up the stairs to the library activity room. We'd signed up to attend a craft class, and I was going to sport my improved attitude. As we rounded the corner, I made sure that I looked approachable. Arms uncrossed. Wide, bright smile as we walked through the door.

A blond woman who I hadn't seen before sat at an oblong table with a tiny, redheaded boy. She smiled back. I noticed her deep dimples and kind, blue eyes. The little boy was about Samuel's age.

There were empty chairs beside her. I decided to walk closer.

"Hi," she said. "I'm Tammy. This is Chase. Do you need a seat? There's one right here."

I sat down next to Tammy. The boys delved into their craft and Tammy and I delved into conversation. Soon class was over, and we still had a lot to say. "Why don't you come over later?" Tammy asked. "I live on a farm. There's plenty of room for the kids to run."

We went.

And since that day, we've been back a million times. Tammy and I became the best of friends, and that farm is like a second home to my boys.

When I look back, I'm grateful for that lonely, tough time. I learned to persevere. I learned to hold my attitude in check. A new sensitivity was born in me — I'm always on the lookout for newcomers. And I was right — I do appreciate my friendship with Tammy. My family has broken into this community, and this little town is where we want to be.

I'm glad I didn't give up.

And as for my boys, they learned a lesson too. A valuable lesson about tough times.

"Keep moving forward," is what I tell them. "Your heart will follow."

And once in a while it leads you.

Straight into the arms of a friend.

~Shawnelle Eliasen

Wake-Up Call

Opening the front door, I heard the piercing sound of an alarm in the darkness.

Hurrying toward the unfamiliar sound, I realized it was the newly installed carbon monoxide detector.

"What color is it blinking?" I asked Mike, my husband.

"Red," he answered. Even before I located the detector's instructions, I knew that couldn't be good.

Maybe that explained why we both hadn't felt well the past couple of days or why my heart suddenly was racing and I was struggling to breathe.

The pamphlet said: "If you hear the alarm horn and the red light is flashing, move everyone to a source of fresh air."

"Call 911," I yelled to Mike, as I opened the front door to let fresh air into the house despite outdoor temperatures in the teens.

Paramedics soon arrived and looked at the carbon monoxide detector and the furnace.

"Usually when we get a call like this the detector is malfunctioning," one of the paramedics said. Suddenly I felt foolish for summoning them on such a cold night. Although I purchased the detector months ago, we'd only had the detector hooked up for a day.

Soon the electric company representative arrived and turned on the furnace, testing the air coming out of several vents. I could hear the rapid beeping of his detector as he leaned over the bedroom vent.

"Sorry folks," he said. "I've got to tag the furnace and turn it off. Levels of carbon monoxide are four times the allowable limits."

We watched in shock as he turned off the pilot light and put a red "notice of improper condition" tag on the gas furnace, which had shown no sign of malfunctioning.

After everyone left, the enormity of the situation sunk in. Chances are, since it was a bitterly cold night, the furnace would have been running more than usual. There was a possibility we might not have made it through the night. If four times the allowable limits of carbon monoxide had seeped into the room in a matter of seconds, how much could have filled the bedroom during the night?

I shuddered to think what could have happened. Christmas was four days away and it was unsettling to think we might not have been alive to celebrate the holiday with my family. Just what, I wondered, had made me decide to install batteries a day ago?

No doubt someone was looking out for us.

Suddenly I had a newfound appreciation for life. I vowed never to take anything for granted again. Even spending a couple of nights in a bone-chillingly cold house until a new furnace was installed was a bearable inconvenience.

After a welcome weeklong vacation at my family's house over the holidays, I returned to work on January fourth, not even dreading the mountain of work awaiting me.

Soon after removing my coat, the newspaper editor summoned me. "Do you have a minute to come with me?" he asked.

As we walked toward the publisher's office, I said, "Uh oh, this isn't good."

"It isn't," he replied. "Layoffs."

We walked in silence, thoughts swirling through my mind. I'd worked at the newspaper for twenty-six years, as an editorial assistant, librarian and now a copy editor. I'd even met my husband here. But I can't say that I didn't think this day would come. I just wasn't expecting it so soon. I knew the newspaper industry was suffering and journalists nationwide were being laid off. I also knew this newspaper was struggling to reinvent itself to remain a community asset. But my role in that reinvention was no longer needed.

As I sat down in the publisher's office, she

handed me a letter and a box of tissues. She explained that the company had eliminated my position due to financial difficulties. My mind tried to process what was happening in between focusing on snippets of conversation: "Joe (the editor) tried every which way to save your job"… "you've always been a good worker"… "have a lot of talent… ."

After returning to my desk, I called my husband, gathered a few belongings and put on my coat. Co-workers came over to hug me as I numbly made my way to the door one last time. I stood outdoors in the blowing snow, waiting for my husband to pick me up. Once settled in the car, I began to cry again.

The rest of the day was a blur, mostly spent fielding phone calls from concerned former co-workers in between bouts of crying. "You're a smart girl, you'll find something else"… "don't worry, you'll be fine"… "you'll find something better" I heard over and over. But the assurance from my former boss that this was a "blessing in disguise" resonated with me. For some inexplicable reason, deep within my consciousness there was a gradual awakening to the notion that this might indeed be a blessing.

The next day, once the initial shock had subsided, I felt like a heavy weight had been lifted. It was an odd, unexpected feeling of liberation, of — dare I say it? — joy. Suddenly, I really, truly realized that the layoff was a blessing … no longer in disguise. Besides, what could possibly be accomplished bemoaning my fate? It was more important to focus on the future.

This, I felt, was a wake-up call: okay, you still have your life. What are you going to do with it? Life's far too brief to be miserable in your career. Although I had worked at the newspaper for more than two decades, it wasn't a job I particularly enjoyed anymore. I was merely going through the motions, pursuing a paycheck. Now was my opportunity to actually work at something I was enthusiastic about.

Years of frugal living had allowed me to

accumulate a financial cushion to see me through some lean times. This safety net further bolstered my determination to take my time embarking on the right career path. Many years ago I realized I could be happy living on much less than most people. Materialism and the endless quest to "keep up with the Joneses," I firmly believed, was no way to live. Becoming mired in burgeoning debt and the endless pursuit of meaningless "things" wasn't living at all. As long as I had shelter, food and a few other basics, I was content.

Since I had always enjoyed the serenity and increased productivity of working from home when I freelanced years ago, it was apparent that that would be a natural choice. The comfort of working from home was something I often missed during my years in a chaotic, noisy, deadline-driven newsroom.

Furthermore, thanks to the Internet, freelance possibilities were endless. I could work for a client hundreds, or thousands, of miles away and instead of being beholden to an employer that often assigned me mind-numbingly dull, creativity-bereft tasks, I would be free to pursue whatever interested me.

Instead of slogging through a pile of work within a strict 9 to 5 schedule, I'd be free to work on my own terms at something more rewarding and fulfilling. As long as I had sufficient income to pay my bills, I didn't even need to return to full-time work. I could spend some of my time volunteering, relaxing or just "being." The choice was mine.

How many times had I heard "do what you love and the money will follow?" Whether it be writing, copyediting, indexing books or selling antiques, I would be doing something — for a change — that I wanted to do in the years remaining until retirement. No doubt it would take hard work and motivation to get established, but I was willing to do whatever was required.

Would I have ever had the courage to quit my job to follow my yearning to be self-employed? Not a chance. Being laid off was the prod I needed to finally follow my heart.

The carbon monoxide scare and a layoff a week later could easily have plunged me into despair. But I recognized it for what it was. Someone was simply trying to send me a message. All I had to do was listen.

~Debbie Dufresne

Meet Our Contributors

Barbara Blossom Ashmun has written six garden books, most recently *Married to My Garden*, about her love affair with plants. She's been writing "Garden Muse," the garden column for the *Portland Tribune* since 2004, and has also contributed to many garden magazines, especially *Fine Gardening*.

Roy A. Barnes writes from southeastern Wyoming. His travel-related works have been published by *Transitions Abroad*, *Travel Thru History*, *In Flight USA*, *Northwest Prime Time*, *Live Life Travel*, *C/Oasis*, BootsnAll.com, and others. His works of poetry and prose have been published by *Poesia*, Skatefic.com, *Literary Liftoff*, *Conceit Magazine* and others.

Debbie Dufresne earned a master's degree in library and information science from Syracuse University. After many years working for a newspaper, she is now a freelance copy editor/proofreader/writer. She is a New York Yankees fan and also enjoys reading and searching for antiques and collectibles at auctions, estate sales and flea markets. E-mail her at Debduf@localnet.com.

Shawnelle Eliasen and her husband Lonny raise their five boys in an old Victorian on the Mississippi River. Her work has been published in *Guideposts*, *Angels on Earth*, *Marriage Partnership*, *MomSense*, *Hearts at Home* magazine, Ourprayer.org, and several anthologies including *Chicken Soup for the Soul*, *Christmas Miracles*, and *Praying from the Heart*.

Inspired by her grandmother, **Kris Flaa** obtained an M.A. in Gerontology before she left corporate management to write, see the National Parks, and spend more time with her family and friends. She recently completed her first novel and lives near Minneapolis with her partner and their charming Westie. E-mail her atkmflaa@comcast.net.

Melanie Adams Hardy received her BS with honors from Spring Hill College in 1984, and her JD from Concord University in 2007. She is an attorney and works for Cunningham Lindsey USA. Melanie enjoys cooking, Pilates, volunteering, and spending time with her husband and children. Please e-mail her at rhardy212@charter.net.

Maggie Koller is a high school teacher in Charlotte, NC, a graduate of Eastern Michigan University, and was previously published in *Chicken Soup for the Soul*. She thanks her mom for telling her to write this story down, and her students who hear this story every year. Please e-mail her at scrappymags@yahoo.com.

Saralee Perel is an award-winning columnist/novelist and multiple contributor to *Chicken Soup for the Soul*. Her book, *The Dog Who Walked Me*, is about her dog who became her caregiver after Saralee's spinal cord injury, the initial devastation of her marriage, and her cat who kept her sane. Contact her at sperel@saraleeperel.com or www.saraleeperel.com.

Theresa Sanders is honored to be a frequent *Chicken Soup for the Soul* contributor. An award-winning technical writer, she managed a documentation and training department before turning to creative endeavors. She lives with her husband near St. Louis, where she is completing a novel. Theresa welcomes e-mails at TheresaLSanders@charter.net.

Tom Schumm is an inspirational speaker who received a BA from Alma College, and an MBA from the University of Michigan. He enjoys boating, travel, opera, and collecting antique fruit jars. He is currently writing a book about his journey with brain cancer. Please e-mail him at tomschumm.pma@gmail.com.

Meet Our Authors

Jack Canfield is the co-creator of the *Chicken Soup for the Soul* series, which *Time* magazine has called "the publishing phenomenon of the decade." Jack is also the co-author of many other bestselling books.

Jack is the CEO of the Canfield Training Group in Santa Barbara, California, and founder of the Foundation for Self-Esteem in Culver City, California. He has conducted intensive personal and professional development seminars on the principles of success for more than a million people in twenty-three countries, has spoken to hundreds of thousands of people at more than 1,000 corporations, universities, professional conferences and conventions, and has been seen by millions more on national television shows.

Jack has received many awards and honors,

including three honorary doctorates and a Guinness World Records Certificate for having seven books from the *Chicken Soup for the Soul* series appearing on the *New York Times* bestseller list on May 24, 1998.

You can reach Jack at
www.jackcanfield.com.

Mark Victor Hansen is the co-founder of Chicken Soup for the Soul, along with Jack Canfield. He is a sought-after keynote speaker, bestselling author, and marketing maven. Mark's powerful messages of possibility, opportunity, and action have created powerful change in thousands of organizations and millions of individuals worldwide.

Mark is a prolific writer with many bestselling books in addition to the *Chicken Soup for the Soul* series. Mark has had a profound influence in the field of human potential through his library of audios, videos, and articles in the areas of big thinking, sales achievement, wealth building, publishing success, and personal and professional development. He is also the founder of the MEGA Seminar Series.

Mark has received numerous awards that honor his entrepreneurial spirit, philanthropic heart, and business acumen. He is a lifetime member of the Horatio Alger Association of Distinguished Americans.

You can reach Mark at
www.markvictorhansen.com.

Amy Newmark was a writer, speaker, Wall Street analyst and business executive in the worlds of finance and telecommunications for more than thirty years. Today she is publisher, editor-in-chief and coauthor of the Chicken Soup for the Soul book series. By curating and editing inspirational true stories from ordinary people who have had extraordinary experiences, Amy has kept the twenty-one-year-old Chicken Soup for the Soul brand fresh and relevant, and still part of the social zeitgeist.

Amy graduated *magna cum laude* from Harvard University where she majored in Portuguese and minored in French. She wrote her thesis about popular, spoken-word poetry in Brazil, which involved traveling throughout Brazil and meeting with poets and writers to collect their stories. She is delighted to have come full circle in her writing career—from collecting poetry "from the people" in Brazil as a twenty-year-old to, three decades later, collecting stories and poems "from the people" for Chicken Soup for the Soul.

Amy has a national syndicated newspaper column and is a frequent radio and TV guest, passing along the real-life lessons and useful tips she has picked up from reading and editing thousands of Chicken Soup for the Soul stories.

She and her husband are the proud parents of four grown children and in her limited spare time, Amy enjoys visiting them, hiking, and reading books that she did not have to edit.

Sharing Happiness, Inspiration, and Wellness

Real people sharing real stories, every day, all over the world. In 2007, *USA Today* named *Chicken Soup for the Soul* one of the five most memorable books in the last quarter-century. With over 100 million books sold to date in the U.S. and Canada alone, more than 200 titles in print, and translations into more than forty languages, "chicken soup for the soul" is one of the world's best-known phrases.

Today, twenty-one years after we first began sharing happiness, inspiration and wellness through our books, we continue to delight our readers with new titles, but have also evolved beyond the bookstore, with wholesome and balanced pet food, delicious nutritious comfort food, and a major motion picture in development. Whatever you're doing, wherever you are, Chicken Soup for the Soul is "always there for you™." Thanks for reading!

Share with Us

We all have had Chicken Soup for the Soul moments in our lives. If you would like to share your story or poem with millions of people around the world, go to chickensoup.com and click on "Submit Your Story." You may be able to help another reader, and become a published author at the same time. Some of our past contributors have launched writing and speaking careers from the publication of their stories in our books!

We only accept story submissions via our website. They are no longer accepted via mail or fax.

To contact us regarding other matters, please send us an e-mail through webmaster@chickensoupforthesoul.com, or fax or write us at:

Chicken Soup for the Soul
P.O. Box 700
Cos Cob, CT 06807-0700
Fax: 203-861-7194

One more note from your friends at Chicken Soup for the Soul: Occasionally, we receive an unsolicited book manuscript from one of our readers, and we would like to respectfully inform you that we do not accept unsolicited manuscripts and we must discard the ones that appear.